Praise for Let Us Pray

"This book is special. It is made for people who have a disability to make it as easy as possible to pray. I hope it helps you become a person who prays, who has the habit of praying, and who enjoys the fruits—the benefits—of prayer in your daily life."

—Archbishop Joseph E. Kurtz, Archbishop
   Emeritus of Louisville, from the foreword

"Let Us Pray is a beautiful collection that encourages readers of all abilities to form a habit of prayer. The introduction defines prayer and describes our practices, appropriately setting the stage for any reader. The subsequent pages are filled with prayers offered in both full and simplified versions to meet the needs of all users. In addition, there are embedded descriptions of potentially difficult words to ensure access to understanding and opportunity for its use. This prayer book is a gift to our Catholic community. It is an intentional and thoughtful reminder that we are all one Body in Christ. All are welcome, especially in prayer!"

—Christie Bonfiglio, Director of the Program for
   Inclusive Education (PIE), University of Notre Dame

"Bishop Robert Barron often reminds us that Jesus' identification with the childlike is preserved in so many of the Gospels because it gets us close to the heart of Jesus' life and message. This book of prayers by Mark Bradford helps to bring all of us into that intimate circle of Jesus' friends. The prayers here are for all of us."

—Archbishop Charles J. Chaput, OFM Cap.,
  Archbishop Emeritus of Philadelphia

"Let Us Pray is a good classic prayer book with the most common Catholic prayers. At the same time, it is a prayer book adapted for people of different abilities, offering explanations of prayer and large type. I appreciate it and I think many others will too."

—Fr. Matthew P. Schneider, LC, author of
  God Loves the Autistic Mind: Prayer Guide for
  Those on the Spectrum and Those Who Love Us

"With great sensitivity and simplicity, Mark Bradford has given us a beautiful book on prayer that people of all ages and abilities can turn to again and again. I can think of no greater contribution a person could make to the disability community than to offer a book that helps readers lift their hearts to God!"

—Charleen Katra, Executive Director, National
  Catholic Partnership on Disability

Let Us Pray

Let Us Pray

Catholic Prayers for All Abilities

Mark Bradford

Foreword by
Archbishop Joseph E. Kurtz

Acknowledgments

A very special thanks to Dr. Brian Skotko, and to Andy and Ben Majewski, Brendan Durkin, Brian Heffernan, and Brendan Whalen, for their willingness to review the text and suggest improvements from their professional and personal experience living and working with people blessed with an extra chromosome.

Published by Word on Fire, Elk Grove Village, IL 60007
© 2025 by Word on Fire Catholic Ministries
Printed in the United States of America
All rights reserved

Art direction and cover design by Katherine Spitler and Rozann Lee.
Typesetting and interior design by 2K/DENMARK.

Scripture excerpts are from the New Revised Standard Version Bible: Catholic Edition (copyright © 1989, 1993), used by permission of the National Council of the Churches of Christ in the United States of America. All rights reserved worldwide.

The Grace Typeface, designed for inclusive reading, has been developed by 2K/DENMARK in collaboration with Cambridge University's Research Department. This innovative typeface is meticulously crafted to enhance readability and comprehension for individuals with dyslexia and other reading challenges.

The type design shows gravity to the baseline, and the letter design is made to achieve the maximum variations to create beautiful words that are easier to read and remember. To achieve the best reading experience for dyslexic readers, there is neither italic nor semi-bold typeface, which would distract the reader. At the same time, the Grace Typeface design rules were adapted to prevent long pieces of text, meaning no paragraphs exceed eleven lines. This is done by imposing a blank line to divide the original manuscript. In these cases, a short dash has been inserted.

In essence, the Grace Typeface transcends conventional typography by prioritizing inclusivity and accessibility without compromising aesthetic appeal. Its thoughtful design empowers individuals of all abilities to engage with written content more effectively, fostering a more inclusive reading experience for diverse audiences worldwide.

ISBN: 978-1-68578-169-9

Library of Congress Control Number: 2024946995

For Thomas Augustine,
and all those with "something extra . . ."

Contents

Foreword 8

Introduction 11

Part 1: Making a Habit of Prayer 19
   The Big Three Catholic Prayers 20
   Prayers for Morning 22
   Prayers for Breakfast, Lunch, and Dinner 26
   Prayers for Bedtime 30

Part 2: Getting More Involved at Sunday Mass . . 35
   Sunday Is Mass Day 36

Part 3: Devotions 47
   The Rosary 48
   The Divine Mercy Chaplet 58
   Adoration of the Blessed Sacrament 64

Part 4: Prayers for Special Times 69
   Prayers to the Blessed Virgin Mary 70
   Prayers to Saint Joseph 76
   Prayers for Your Family 80
   Prayers for Your Life's Purpose 84
   Prayers for Priests 88
   Prayers for People with Disabilities 92
   Prayers When You or Someone Else Is Sick 96
   Prayers to End Abortion 100
   Prayers When Someone You Love Has Died or Is Dying . . 104

Notes 109
Image Credits 112

Foreword
Archbishop Joseph E. Kurtz

When I first went to school to learn to be a priest about sixty years ago, I went to the chapel for my first Sunday Mass and saw that the Sunday prayer book was gigantic. It must have had two thousand pages and at least fifteen bookmarks to keep track of where I was supposed to pray. The book had a Latin name: the Liber Usualis (though it was anything but a usual book of prayer). I looked around and saw that the other seminarians knew exactly what to do. They could turn those pages better than I could drive a car. Was I ever going to learn to pray?

I finally learned how to use that big book, but more important than that, I learned that prayer was about talking with God, who loves me so much. I also learned that prayer is meant for every one of us. And I found that there is such a thing as a habit of praying. The more you pray, the more likely you'll continue to pray.

Most importantly, I learned what happened to me when I prayed. When I prayed, I felt closer to God. I trusted more in God's love and plan for me, and I began to realize that prayer is not just about asking for something; it is also giving praise and thanks to God for what he has already done for me. Finally, I realized that if I learned some of the prayers in that big book, I would be able to join with others in prayer in community.

Mark Bradford has prepared this wonderful and simple book on prayer, Let Us Pray: Catholic Prayers for All Abilities, and it is a book that everyone can use.

My older brother George loved to pray and go to Mass.
He was five years older than me and was born with
Down syndrome. Even though he couldn't read as well as
everybody else in our family, he learned certain prayers
and could recite them from memory. He also became so
familiar with the words of the Our Father that he could say
them when we went to Sunday Mass, when we said our
prayers at night, or when we were about to have a meal.

This book is special. It is made for people who have a disability
to make it as easy as possible to pray. I hope it helps you
become a person who prays, who has the habit of praying, and
who enjoys the fruits—the benefits—of prayer in your daily life.

Please use this beautiful gift with the right attitude. Jesus
teaches us about the right attitude. Once, he described a very
proud man who was very successful in life. He loved to sit in
the first pew at church and brag to God about what a good
man he was. Jesus compared him to another man who was
in the very back of the church with his head bowed—humbly
praying as one who is not perfect. This man was a tax collector,
and people then didn't like tax collectors very much. Jesus
praised the tax collector because he prayed with humility
and was very open to trusting in God's mercy. I don't know
about you, but I'd like to be more like that tax collector who
really knows what it means to be humble and trust in God.

Finally, don't forget to pray for others. Learning formal
prayers like the Our Father—the prayer Jesus taught us—helps
us remember that we don't bring only our own needs and
desires to God. We are all a part of God's family, so we pray
for others, remembering that others are praying for us too.

Introduction

This book is offered by Word on Fire primarily to adults who are living with an intellectual disability, but others may enjoy it too. Its purpose is to encourage people to form a habit of prayer.

What is prayer? It is talking with God and thinking about him and others with compassion, forgiveness, gratitude, and thanksgiving. And most of all, it is about love—our love for God and our love for our families and friends.

Everyone can pray. It's simple. God loves you and wants to hear from you. He loves everyone, and he wants you to love him too. The best way to show him we love him is to spend time with him.

Prayer isn't hard. It is as simple as having a heart-to-heart conversation with God. Sometimes we pray with words and sometimes without words. In fact, just thinking about God can be a prayer.

As Catholics, we always begin to pray with the sign of the cross. It's a way of starting our conversation with God—kind of like saying "Hello!" We say:

> In the name of the Father, and of the
> Son, and of the Holy Spirit.

When we begin our prayer this way, it reminds us that we know God in three ways: as Father, Son, and Holy Spirit. That's kind of hard to understand, but don't worry. Just think about these three ways we can think of God.

A Symbol of the Holy Spirit

How would you imagine something you can't see? We can't see the Holy Spirit, but we use symbols for him. One of those is a dove. The gentle dove makes us think of peace, and its white color makes us think of purity. When Jesus was baptized by John the Baptist, the Bible tells us that the Holy Spirit came down from heaven in the form of a dove.

God as Our Father, Our Creator

We can talk with God like we would talk with our father. We can tell him how amazed we are at all he has done for us: for creating our beautiful world and for sending his Son, Jesus, to show us how much he loves us.

God as Jesus, Our Brother

For some people it is easier to talk with Jesus. He is God's Son, who became a human being just like us, except he is also God. We can talk with him like we would talk with a friend. We can see him in our imagination with images from the Bible—images like when he was a small baby in the manger at Christmas, or when he asked that all the little children be brought to him. We can see him on the cross and be thankful that he suffered and died for us to save us from sin and show us how very much God loves us. We can have no better friend.

God as the Holy Spirit, Our Helper

Some people like to pray to the Holy Spirit and ask him to increase his gifts in us. The Holy Spirit lives in each of us through our Baptism. When we have trouble praying, Saint Paul told us that we can ask the Holy Spirit to help us. He will even pray for us when we can't find the words to use! Just ask.

Praying to Mary, Our Mother

We have lots of friends in heaven. We call them saints. Jesus' mother is a very special saint. She is not God, but she is a very special friend whom we can ask to pray for us. We call her the Blessed Virgin Mary, our mother in heaven. Remember the Bible story of the wedding feast that ran out of wine? She asked Jesus to turn water into wine, and he did!

God and the Saints Are Our Friends

Friends are important to God, just like they are to us. When two friends talk with each other, they know it is as important to listen to their friend as it is to speak. When we pray, we talk with God, and sometimes he speaks to us too, in our hearts. It's as simple as that.

If you have trouble praying, you don't need to use a lot of words. You can say short prayers like this one by Saint Gemma Galgani:

My God, my God, I love you.

Or like Saint Faustina:

Jesus, I trust in you.

Here is one more very simple prayer. It's drawn from the Bible, and some people never stop saying it. They say it has changed their lives. It's called the Jesus Prayer, and it goes like this:

Lord Jesus Christ, Son of God,
    have mercy on me, a sinner.

There are many short prayers like these in this book. They are easy to remember so you can pray them at any time of the day, or even if you are lying awake in your bed at night.

Sacred Heart

Our hearts are a very special place. When we are sad, we might say we have a broken heart, or when we're very happy we might say, "I feel like my heart will burst." Jesus' heart burns with love for us, and the image of his heart—his Sacred Heart—surrounded by his crown of thorns reminds us that he loves us so much he died for us.

The main thing God wants of us when we
pray is what he tells us in the Psalms: "Be still,
and know that I am God!" (Psalm 46:10).

We hope this book helps you be still with God.
The more we get to know him, the happier we will be,
and others around us will be too. Prayer helps us know
God better and will help others see God's love in us.

How to Use This Book

Some people love to pray, and others find it hard
to pray. Some may have never even tried to pray.
We hope this book helps everyone pray more.

If you don't pray very much, or have never prayed,
maybe a good way to start is to pray before you eat your
meals. There is a simple prayer most Catholics know
and can pray together that you will find on page 28.
Of course, you can pray in your own words too.

The first part of this book has basic Catholic prayers that
you can use to pray all throughout the day. Everything is
easier when it becomes a habit. Why not make a habit of
talking with God and our Blessed Mother, Mary, every day?

Since some people are better at reading than
others, there are some very simple prayers in this
book and some that may be harder. Skip the ones
that are too hard. Remember that you can pray in
your own words or write your own prayers too.

We hope this book will help you begin a
good new habit of praying every day!

Other Parts of This Book

Part 2 has prayers that you might want to pray at Mass on Sunday. They will help you become better at participating in the Mass.

Part 3 has three devotions that are very popular: the Rosary, the Divine Mercy Chaplet, and Adoration of Jesus in the Blessed Sacrament.

Part 4 has prayers that you might want to pray if you're sick, or sad, or wondering what God wants you to do with your life.

It is important to develop a way to pray that you enjoy so you can grow in your friendship with God.

Part 1

Making a Habit of Prayer

The Big Three Catholic Prayers

If you're not used to praying, that's okay. Now is a good time to start. Here are some simple prayers that you can pray through your day to help you make a habit of praying. You can start with just a few of them, like praying before your meals, and then add more as you want to.

Let's start with the big three Catholic prayers that you may already know. You can pray them anytime or several times through the day. They are also part of other prayers like the Rosary.

Our Father

Our Father, who art in heaven,
hallowed be thy name;
thy kingdom come,
thy will be done
on earth as it is in heaven.
Give us this day our daily bread,
and forgive us our trespasses,
as we forgive those who trespass against us;
and lead us not into temptation,
but deliver us from evil.
Amen.

Hail Mary

Hail Mary, full of grace, the Lord is with thee;
blessed art thou among women,
and blessed is the fruit of thy womb, Jesus.
Holy Mary, Mother of God,
pray for us sinners,
now and at the hour of our death.
Amen.

Glory Be

Glory be to the Father,
    and to the Son,
    and to the Holy Spirit;
as it was in the beginning,
    is now, and ever shall be,
world without end.
Amen.

"Trespasses" are our sins, or things we do wrong.

21

Prayers for Morning

Here is a plan that can help you start praying every day. Again, you can pray all these prayers, or you can just pray the ones you want to pray to start. It's just important to pray! God is waiting to hear from you.

(Remember, you can pray with these prayers, or you can just spend a few minutes praying quietly in your own words. Maybe these prayers will help you get started.) When you wake up, it is good to offer your day to Jesus with a morning prayer.

Morning Prayer

My Jesus, I love you more than anything.
I offer my day to you and ask you to
    show me how to love you more.
Amen.

Or you can pray this:

My Jesus, I offer to you all that I am
    and all that I have today.
I offer to you all that makes me happy
    and any suffering I may have.
I offer everything to your glory, dear Jesus.
I offer myself to your most Sacred Heart
and pray especially for those who have
    left the Roman Catholic Church,
for those in Purgatory,
    for those who don't believe in you,
      —
and for all the sins against your most precious
    Body and Blood in Holy Communion.
I pray for my family and friends,
    for my pastor, my bishop,
    and for the pope.
I pray especially for those who have died
    and for those who will die today.
Amen.

It is also important to remember our mother in heaven,
the Blessed Virgin Mary, who loves us and always
wants to bring us closer to Jesus. You can say the prayer
on the next page to offer your day to her and to ask for
her help through your day.

23

Morning Prayer to Mary

Mother Mary, I am all yours today.
Teach me to love Jesus more.
Amen.

Or you can pray this:

Mary, I offer myself to you and to Jesus today.
To show how much I love you,
I offer to you my eyes to see the beauty around me,
my ears to hear, my mouth to tell
     people I care about them,
my heart to learn how to love more
     and to be kind to others.
Dear Mother, keep me safe today
and protect me from every bad thing.
I am all yours, O Mary.
Amen.

Did you know that God gave you a special angel to protect you through your whole life? This is your very own guardian angel, whom you can pray to often.

Guardian Angel Prayer

Angel of God, my guardian dear,
to whom God's love commits me here.
Ever this day be at my side
to light, to guard, to rule, to guide.
Amen.

Prayers for Breakfast, Lunch, and Dinner

Angelus is a Latin word that means "the angel."

The Angelus is a very special prayer that reminds us of God's gift of his Son, Jesus. Many Catholics pray this prayer three times every day: in the morning, at noon, and again in the evening before dinner. You might start by just praying it at lunchtime.

You can pray the Angelus first, or just thank God for your meal.

The Angelus

The Angel of the Lord declared unto Mary.
—And she conceived of the Holy Spirit.
Hail Mary, full of grace, the Lord is with thee;
blessed art thou among women,
and blessed is the fruit of thy womb, Jesus.
Holy Mary, Mother of God,
pray for us sinners,
now and at the hour of our death.
Amen.

Behold the handmaid of the Lord,
—Be it done unto me according to Thy Word.

Pray the Hail Mary just like before.

Bow or kneel.

And the Word was made flesh.
—And dwelt among us.

Rise, and pray the Hail Mary again.

Pray for us, O holy Mother of God,
—that we may be made worthy of the promises of Christ.

Pour forth, we beseech thee, O Lord,
    thy grace into our hearts,
that we, to whom the Incarnation of Christ thy Son
was made known by the message of an angel,
may by his Passion and Cross
be brought to the glory of his Resurrection.
Through the same Christ our Lord.
Amen.

One of the names for Jesus is "the Word." When we say, "The Word was made flesh," we are just saying that Jesus became a human being like us.

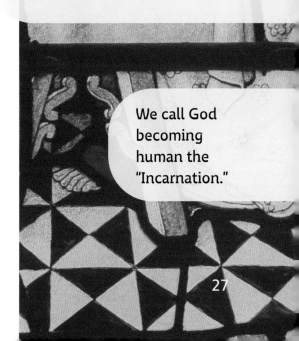

We call God becoming human the "Incarnation."

God is very generous with his gifts. His generosity is his "bounty" that he shares with us.

And don't forget to thank God for your food!

Grace at Meals

Bless us, O Lord, and these your gifts,
which we are about to receive from your bounty,
through Christ our Lord.
Amen.

What would you say to Jesus if you were having breakfast with him?

Prayers for Bedtime

Bedtime is a good time to think about our day and to be thankful to God for all he has done for us. Maybe answer these four questions and then take your answers to God in a short prayer before you go to sleep.

1. What good things happened to you today?

2. What did you do today that would make God happy?

3. Is there anything you did today that would make God sad?

4. Is there anyone that you want to pray for, like your mother, father, or a friend?

After you have thought about these things, you can say "good night" to Jesus in your own words or pray this prayer:

Night Prayer

I thank you, God, that you have loved
   me and kept me safe today.
Please forgive me for whatever I have done wrong
and keep me and those I love safe through this night.
Send my guardian angel to be with me tonight
so that I can sleep well and so that I
   can serve you and love you
more and more tomorrow and forever.
Amen.

Here is a special prayer for bedtime that was given
to us by Saint Augustine a long time ago.

Saint Augustine's Prayer for Bedtime

Watch, Lord, with those who wake or weep tonight.
Ask the angels and saints to watch
   over those who sleep.
O Lord Jesus Christ, tend your sick ones,
   rest your weary ones,
bless your dying ones, soothe the suffering ones,
pity all the afflicted ones, shield the joyful ones,
and all for your love's sake.
Amen.

Psalm 4:8

I will both lie down
   and sleep in peace;
   for you alone, O LORD,
   make me lie down
   in safety.

31

There are a lot more prayers and special devotions that you can pray through the day, like the Rosary and the Divine Mercy Chaplet. You might also have a chance to go to church and pray during a special time of Adoration when Jesus in the Blessed Sacrament is placed on the altar. If you don't know how, you can find out how to pray these prayers beginning on page 48.

Bedtime Moon

Can you see the moon in this picture? It's white and near the stars.

> O God, when I consider the moon and the stars, the wonders you have made, what am I that you think of me? (See Psalm 8)

Part 2

Getting More Involved at Sunday Mass

Sunday Is Mass Day

Sunday is a very special day. We call it the Lord's Day. Jesus rose from the dead on Sunday, and all Catholics are supposed to go to church on Sundays to remember the death and Resurrection of Jesus.

Sometimes Mass may seem boring, but it isn't if you think about the miracle that happens at every Mass. It's like heaven opens up and comes down to us. We are surrounded by angels and saints, and when the priest says the words "This is my Body" and "This is the cup of my Blood," the bread and wine really become the Body and Blood of Jesus!

It is important to pay attention, pray along with the priest, and remember what is happening. Being at Mass is the most important thing we can ever do.

We shouldn't think about what we get out of Mass as much as what Mass is all about. We are going to tell God "Thank you" for the gift of his Son, Jesus, and the sacrifice he made for us so that we can go to heaven.

Maybe this short introduction and these prayers will help.

How to Participate in the Mass

When we come to worship God in the Mass, Jesus gives us his Body and Blood and offers us the strength to face what is hard for us. He is there to help us with our life. At Mass, God reminds us how much he loves us. This is our time to say thank you.

When it is hard to pay attention, try to focus on Jesus and tell him everything you want him to know. You can pray for your family and friends, people you know who are sick or who have died, or maybe friends or family who need your help, or who don't believe in Jesus and his Church.

Maybe these prayers will help you pay attention and participate more at Mass. Don't forget that you can also pray in your own words.

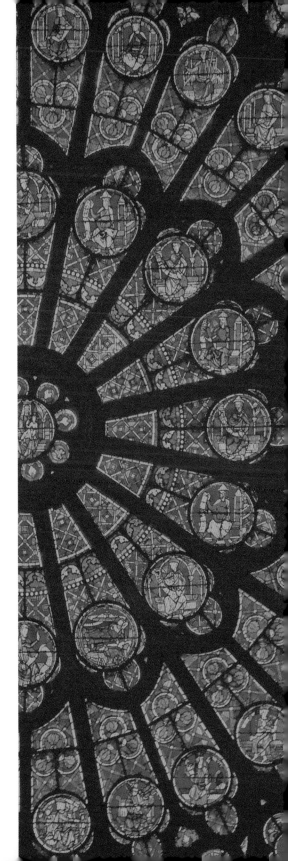

Prayer Before Mass Begins

O my God, I love you so much.
Thank you for Jesus Christ,
who died for us so that we can be close to you,
so close that we become one with
    you in Holy Communion.
I know that soon when I receive his Body and Blood,
Jesus will live in me.
I always want to live for him.
Please help me to pay attention
and to listen to the readings from
    the Bible that I will hear.

    —

Help me to understand what I hear,
but also help me not to be frustrated
    if I don't understand.
I want to receive your Body and Blood
so that I can love you more
and do whatever you want me to do in this world,
and especially in your Church.
I bring to you all the needs of all
    my family and friends,
and especially (add your own prayers here).
Amen.

Or you can pray this:

I am yours, my Jesus.
Make my heart like your Heart
    —filled with love for you
    and your people.
Amen.

Or this:

My God, I love you.
Thank you for Jesus, your Son,
whom I have come to worship and receive here.
I want to give to you all that I am and all
    that I have in this Holy Mass.
Help me to pay attention.
Please forgive me for any way I have made you sad
so that I can receive Jesus in the best
    way in Holy Communion.
Amen.

Prayer at the Readings

Jesus, your words from the Bible help me know
how to live better and how to love you more.
Help me listen carefully and
    understand the best I can.
When I don't understand, please
    teach me in my heart
how to love and serve you better.
Amen.

Prayer When the Gifts Are Brought to the Altar

My Lord, Jesus Christ,
I offer you all the feelings of my heart.
All I can give to you is my heart,
and all the things that make me happy,
and even the things that make me
      sad or that hurt me.
I bring the things I might have done
      that hurt you,
and want to tell you I am sorry.
I pray especially for
      (add all of your special prayers here).
      —

I offer to you all that I am and have.
Please teach me to love you more
and to use my life to help others
      love you more too.
Amen.

Or you can pray this:

My Jesus, I offer you all that I am and have.
Everything I have is your gift to me.
Teach me to use them to bring you glory.
Your grace and your love are all that I need.
Please, my Jesus, give me only these things.
All I need is you.
Amen.

Prayer After You Receive Holy Communion

Soul of Christ, make me holy.
Body of Christ, save me.
Blood of Christ, satisfy my desire for you.
Water from the side of Christ, wash away my sins.
Passion of Christ, make me strong.
Good and gentle Jesus, hear me.
Within your wounds, hide me
and protect me from every bad thing.

—

When it is time for me to die, call me
and welcome me to be with you in heaven,
so that I can praise you with all your saints
for ever and ever.
Amen.

Psalm 34:8

O taste and see that
    the Lord is good;
    happy are those
    who take refuge in him.

Saying Thank You to Jesus After Mass

My Jesus, I have heard your word
and received your Body and Blood
    in Holy Communion.
I love you and thank you for this
    time I have had with you.
Please make me strong and joyful.
Help me remember to praise you
and be grateful to you every day in my heart.
Help me remember that when I leave this church
you will stay with me as my friend
    through each day of my life.
        —

Help me to remember this gift I have received.
I want to come back soon to receive you once again.
Until then, I will hold you close to my heart.
Jesus, I love you.
Amen.

Or you can pray this:

My God, thank you for Jesus
and for this time I have had to be with
    you and to worship you.
Thank you for all you have done for me.
Amen.

Prayers to Become a Better Person

You can also pray these prayers at Mass. When we receive Holy Communion, we grow to be more like Jesus, with a stronger faith and hope in what he has promised us and with a stronger love for God and one another.

A Simple Act of Faith, Hope, and Love

My God,
I believe all that you have taught
    us with all my heart.
I hope to spend eternity with you in heaven,
and I love you more than anything.
Help me to grow in faith, hope, and love
so that I can love you more and
    become more like you.
Amen.

Act of Faith

O my God, I firmly believe
that you are one God in three divine Persons,
Father, Son, and Holy Spirit.
I believe that your divine Son became man
and died for our sins and that he will come
to judge the living and the dead.
I believe these and all the truths
which the Holy Catholic Church teaches
because you have revealed them
who are eternal truth and wisdom,
who can neither deceive nor be deceived.
In this faith I intend to live and die.
Amen.

Act of Hope

O Lord God,
I hope by your grace for the pardon
of all my sins
and after life here to gain eternal happiness
because you have promised it
who are infinitely powerful, faithful, kind,
and merciful.
In this hope I intend to live and die.
Amen.

Act of Love

O Lord God, I love you above all things
and I love my neighbor for your sake
because you are the highest, infinite and perfect
good, worthy of all my love.
In this love I intend to live and die.
Amen.

Rosary Lily

These white flowers on the Bible are
lilies. A lily is a symbol of love and
goodness. When we pray, God fills
us with love and helps us be good.

Psalm 25:4

Make me to know
 your ways, O Lᴏʀᴅ;
 teach me your paths.

Part 3

Devotions

The Rosary

The Rosary is a very special gift from our mother, Mary. Maybe you already pray the Rosary. If not, it is easy, and now is a great time to start. It's a prayer that anyone can pray with just a little practice.

If you want, you can pray the Rosary on YouTube with Bishop Barron or others. Just search for it. It's easy to find. Go to YouTube and type "Bishop Barron Joyful (or Sorrowful, or Glorious, or Luminous) Mysteries." Or even just type "Pray the Rosary." Easy!

Praying the Rosary takes about twenty minutes, but you don't have to pray the whole thing. You can start by only praying one of the mysteries, like the Annunciation.

Just think about this one mystery and pray one Our Father, ten Hail Marys, a Glory Be, and the Fatima Prayer (see below). You can add more mysteries when you want to.

You can pray the Rosary alone or with others. Don't forget that you can pray for someone who is sick, or your family, or even those who say they aren't Catholic anymore. Pray especially for them! You can pray to ask Mary to help you be stronger and more faithful, or to give you strength when you feel weak, afraid, or sick. The Rosary is a beautiful prayer!

The Rosary is divided into four parts that help us think about different parts of Jesus' life. We call these parts "mysteries." We usually pray the mysteries on certain days of the week, but you can really pray them anytime. Each of these mysteries has five different parts that help us think about different times in the life of Jesus. They are:

The Joyful Mysteries

(Pray on Monday and Saturday)

In these mysteries, we remember the gift of Jesus being born as a tiny baby. God became a human being, just like us. The world was changed forever.

"There is no problem, I tell you, no matter how difficult it is, that we cannot solve by the prayer of the Holy Rosary."

—Sister Lucia, one of the children at Fatima

"When you say your Rosary, the angels rejoice, the Blessed Trinity delights in it, my Son, Jesus, finds joy in it too, and I myself am happier than you can possibly guess. After the Holy Sacrifice of the Mass, there is nothing in the Church that I love as much as the Rosary."

—Mary to Blessed Alan de la Roche

The angel Gabriel came to Mary to ask her if she would be Jesus' mother. Hail Mary, full of grace!

The Annunciation: The angel Gabriel comes to Mary to tell her that God chose her to be the mother of his Son, Jesus. She says, "Let it be with me according to your word" (Luke 1:38), and she becomes pregnant by a miracle of the Holy Spirit.

The Visitation: Mary goes to visit her cousin Elizabeth, who is pregnant with John the Baptist. Elizabeth knows Mary is pregnant with Jesus and greets her as the mother of her Lord. Her baby, John the Baptist, leaps for joy in her womb. Mary prays her Magnificat: "My soul magnifies the Lord, and my spirit rejoices in God my savior" (Luke 1:46–47).

The Nativity: Jesus is born in Bethlehem, and the shepherds and angels are all gathered around him singing and rejoicing. "God's love was revealed among us in this way: God sent his only Son into the world so that we might live through him" (1 John 4:9).

The Presentation in the Temple: Jews took their new babies to the temple to say thank you to God. Mary and Joseph are Jewish and take Jesus to the temple to present him to God. Two special older people are there, Simeon and Anna. They know that Jesus is the Messiah, the "Glory of Israel" and the "Light to the Nations."

The Finding in the Temple: On their way home from Jerusalem, Mary and Joseph realize that Jesus isn't with them. They go back and find him teaching in the temple. He says to them, "Did you not know that I must be in my Father's house?" (Luke 2:49). Even as a young boy, Jesus knew that his mission was to do what his Father had sent him to do.

The Sorrowful Mysteries

(Pray on Tuesday and Friday)

In these mysteries, we remember how Jesus suffered and died to save us from our sins and show us the way to heaven.

The Agony in the Garden: Jesus prays alone in the garden before he is taken by the soldiers and put on the cross. He is afraid and prays that, if it is God's will, he will not have to suffer. But he knows that his death was the reason for his birth. He had come to suffer and die for us, to save us from our sin.

The Scourging at the Pillar: Jesus is tied to a post and whipped by the soldiers until he almost dies. He does all this because he loves us. He suffers to save us from our sins.

The Crowning with Thorns: The soldiers make fun of Jesus. They don't believe that he is the King of the universe. They put a crown of thorns on his head and tease him about being a king.

The Carrying of the Cross: Jesus carries his heavy cross to the place where he will die. Some special people help him along the way, and others tease him. We should help Jesus carry his cross by helping others whenever we can.

The Crucifixion and Death: Jesus dies on the cross. His mission on earth is finished. From the cross, he gives Mary to us as our mother. When he dies, the world gets dark and there are earthquakes. Jesus' death on the cross changes the world forever.

The cross always reminds us of how much Jesus suffered for us. When we see it, we can thank him for what he did. By his suffering he saved us and helps us get to heaven.

The Glorious Mysteries

(Pray on Wednesday and Sunday)

In these mysteries, we think about Easter, Pentecost, and how Jesus rewarded Mary for saying yes to becoming his mother.

The Resurrection: Jesus' friends go to visit his grave early on Easter morning, but he is not there. He has risen from the dead, just like he said he would.

The Ascension: Jesus spends forty days on earth after his Resurrection. Before he ascends (goes up) into heaven, he tells his Apostles that the Holy Spirit will come to guide the Church and be with it forever, until the end of the world.

The Descent of the Holy Spirit: Just as Jesus promised, the Holy Spirit comes to the Apostles on Pentecost. The Bible says he came like a rushing wind and with tongues of fire. Pentecost is the Church's birthday.

The Assumption: Jesus loved his mother very much. When she told the angel Gabriel that she would do whatever God wanted and gave birth to Jesus, she did something no other human would ever do. Rather than allow her to be buried in a grave, Jesus takes her to be with him in heaven. She is there right now praying for us.

The Coronation of Mary: Jesus is our King, and his mother, Mary, is our Queen. She said yes to God and has been given great power to help Jesus bring all of us to heaven when we die.

The Luminous Mysteries, or the Mysteries of Light

(Pray on Thursday)

In these mysteries, we think about what Jesus did when he was with us on earth, and how he came to live with us and to teach us the way to heaven.

The Baptism of Christ in the Jordan: When John the Baptist sees Jesus coming to him to be baptized, he says, "Here is the Lamb of God who takes away the sin of the world!" (John 1:29). The priest says those very words at Mass.

The Wedding Feast at Cana: Jesus works his first miracle by turning water into wine at Cana. Why? Because his mother asks him to. We can remember how close Jesus and Mary are, and when we pray to Mary, we know that she will ask Jesus to help us.

Jesus' Proclamation of the Coming of the Kingdom of God: Jesus came to show us how much God loves us. The Gospels tell us stories of Jesus' teaching so that we know how to live and learn to love him more.

The Transfiguration: Jesus goes up a high mountain with three of his closest friends and lets them see his glory as God. It helps them believe even more that he really is God's Son.

The Institution of the Eucharist: The Holy Eucharist is our greatest gift. In it we receive the Body, Blood, Soul, and Divinity of Jesus. It is his special gift to help us receive eternal life.

So, now you're ready! Praying with others is a good way to begin. This is how you pray the Rosary.

Jesus did his first miracle at a wedding in Cana. They had run out of wine, so he turned water into wine for their party.

The Rosary

Begin with the sign of the cross:

> In the name of the Father, and of the
> Son, and of the Holy Spirit.

Hold the crucifix and pray the Apostles' Creed.
If you want, you can skip this prayer
and go right to the Our Father.

> I believe in God,
> the Father almighty,
> Creator of heaven and earth,
> and in Jesus Christ, his only Son, our Lord,
> who was conceived by the Holy Spirit,
> born of the Virgin Mary,
> suffered under Pontius Pilate,
> was crucified, died, and was buried;
> he descended into hell;
> on the third day he rose again from the dead;
>   —
> he ascended into heaven,
> and is seated at the right hand of
>   God the Father almighty;
> from there he will come to judge
>   the living and the dead.

> I believe in the Holy Spirit,
> the holy catholic Church,
> the communion of saints,
> the forgiveness of sins,
> the resurrection of the body,
> and life everlasting.
> Amen.

On the first bead, pray an Our Father:

> Our Father, who art in heaven,
> hallowed be thy name;
> thy kingdom come,
> thy will be done
> on earth as it is in heaven.
> Give us this day our daily bread,
> and forgive us our trespasses,
> as we forgive those who trespass against us;
> and lead us not into temptation,
> but deliver us from evil.
> Amen.

On the next three beads, pray a Hail Mary:

> Hail Mary, full of grace, the Lord is with thee;
> blessed art thou among women,
> and blessed is the fruit of thy womb, Jesus.
> Holy Mary, Mother of God,
> pray for us sinners,
> now and at the hour of our death.
> Amen.

On the next bead, pray a Glory Be:

> Glory be to the Father, and to the
>   Son, and to the Holy Spirit;
> as it was in the beginning, is now, and ever shall be,
> world without end.
> Amen.

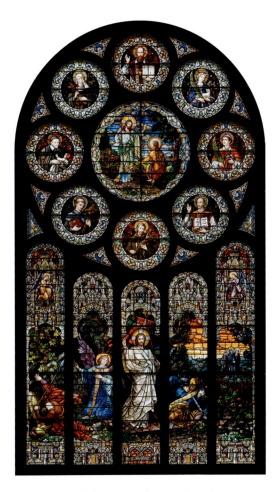

This beautiful image shows the glory of Jesus rising from the dead. See all the saints who surround him? Like them, our lives can be changed by thinking about the Resurrection.

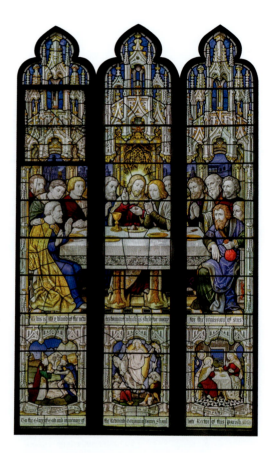

This is a picture of the Last Supper when Jesus gave us the Eucharist. Do you remember Judas was there? Can you guess which one of the men is him?

Pray the first mystery from the Joyful, Sorrowful, Glorious, or Luminous Mysteries.

1. On the large bead, announce the mystery and then say an Our Father.

2. On each of the ten small beads, say a Hail Mary while continuing to meditate on the mystery.

3. At the end of the ten Hail Marys, say the Glory Be.

4. Then say the Fatima Prayer:

> O my Jesus, forgive us our sins,
>   save us from the fires of hell;
> lead all souls to heaven, especially those
>   who have most need of thy mercy.
> Amen.

Do the same thing for each of the mysteries that you're praying: Our Father, ten Hail Marys, Glory Be, Fatima Prayer. After you finish praying all five mysteries, then pray the Hail, Holy Queen:

> Hail, holy Queen, Mother of Mercy,
> our life, our sweetness, and our hope.
> To thee do we cry, poor banished children of Eve;
> to thee do we send up our sighs,
> mourning and weeping in this valley of tears.
> Turn, then, most gracious advocate,
> thine eyes of mercy toward us;
>
> —
>
> and after this, our exile,
> show unto us the blessed fruit of thy womb, Jesus.
> O clement, O loving, O sweet Virgin Mary.
> Pray for us, O holy Mother of God,
> that we may be made worthy of the promises of Christ.

Finish with the final prayer:

> Let us pray.
> O God, whose only begotten Son,
> by his life, death, and Resurrection,
> has purchased for us the rewards of eternal life,
> grant, we beseech thee,
> that while meditating on these mysteries
> of the most holy Rosary of the Blessed Virgin Mary,
> we may imitate what they contain
> and obtain what they promise,
> through the same Christ our Lord.
> Amen.

End with the sign of the cross.

(Optional: some people end by praying the Prayer to Saint Michael after the sign of the cross.)

> Saint Michael the Archangel,
> defend us in battle.
> Be our protection against the wickedness
>   and snares of the devil.
> —
> May God rebuke him, we humbly pray,
> and do thou,
> O Prince of the heavenly hosts,
> by the power of God,
> cast into hell Satan,
> and all the evil spirits,
> who prowl about the world
> seeking the ruin of souls.
> Amen.

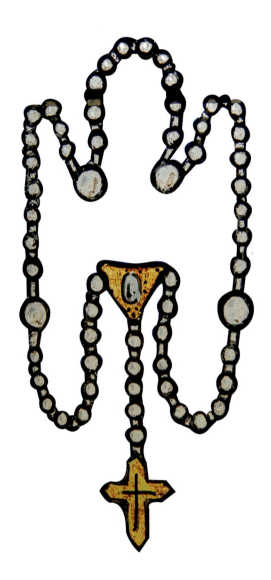

The Divine Mercy Chaplet

A long time ago, a young girl entered a convent in Poland to become a nun and became known as Sister Maria Faustina of the Most Blessed Sacrament. She had a very special relationship with Jesus. She loved him so much that he eventually asked her to tell everyone about his mercy—his "Divine Mercy."

Jesus asked Sister Faustina to write down everything he said to her. Among his many words was a very beautiful prayer that Jesus gave to us to pray. It is the Divine Mercy Chaplet.

What is the Divine Mercy? It is God's love reaching out to us to help us through things that are hard for us. He wants to help us with our weaknesses, problems in our family, and everything that you can think of that makes your life hard.

Jesus made many promises to people who would pray this beautiful prayer. It is a very powerful prayer to pray when someone is sick or dying: "For the sake of his sorrowful Passion, have mercy on us and on the whole world."

You can use your rosary to pray the Divine Mercy Chaplet. Some people have a special small rosary with only ten beads.

This is how you pray the Divine Mercy Chaplet. If you want, you can skip the first three prayers and just start with the Eternal Father prayer.

The Divine Mercy Chaplet

Make the sign of the cross with your rosary.

Pray one Our Father:

> Our Father, who art in heaven,
> hallowed be thy name;
> thy kingdom come,
> thy will be done
> on earth as it is in heaven.
> Give us this day our daily bread,
> and forgive us our trespasses,
> as we forgive those who trespass against us;
> and lead us not into temptation,
> but deliver us from evil.
> Amen.

Pray one Hail Mary:

Hail Mary, full of grace, the Lord is with thee;
blessed art thou among women,
and blessed is the fruit of thy womb, Jesus.
Holy Mary, Mother of God,
pray for us sinners,
now and at the hour of our death.
Amen.

Pray the Apostles' Creed:

I believe in God,
the Father almighty,
Creator of heaven and earth,
and in Jesus Christ, his only Son, our Lord,
who was conceived by the Holy Spirit,
born of the Virgin Mary,
suffered under Pontius Pilate,
was crucified, died, and was buried;
he descended into hell;
on the third day he rose again from the dead;
—
he ascended into heaven,
and is seated at the right hand of God
the Father almighty;
from there he will come to judge
the living and the dead.

I believe in the Holy Spirit,
the holy catholic Church,
the communion of saints,
the forgiveness of sins,
the resurrection of the body,
and life everlasting.
Amen.

Before Jesus died on the cross, he prayed in the garden for all of us—even you and me. Remember how the angels came to him? You can see one here.

Holding your rosary, start on the large
bead with the Eternal Father prayer:

> Eternal Father,
> I offer you the Body and Blood, Soul and Divinity
> of your dearly beloved Son, Our Lord Jesus Christ,
> in atonement for our sins and those
>   of the whole world.

Then, say this short prayer on each of
the ten beads of your rosary:

> For the sake of his sorrowful Passion,
> have mercy on us and on the whole world.

Continue praying these prayers around the
five decades of your rosary, and when you
have finished, pray this prayer three times:

> Holy God, Holy Mighty One, Holy Immortal One,
> have mercy on us and on the whole world.

When you have finished these prayers, you
can end with the prayer on the next page.

"Immortal" means
you will never die.
God is the "Immortal One."

There are some hard words here: "compassion" is feeling what someone else feels; "inexhaustible" means it will never run out; "despair" is feeling like you don't have any hope; and "despondent" is being very depressed.

Eternal God,
in whom mercy is endless and the treasury
    of compassion inexhaustible,
look kindly upon us and increase your mercy in us,
that in difficult moments we might not
    despair nor become despondent,
but with great confidence submit
    ourselves to your holy will,
which is love and mercy itself.
Amen.

You can pray the Divine Mercy Chaplet as often as you want. Many people pray it at 3:00 in the afternoon, since that is the time that Jesus died on the cross, but you can pray it any time.

THE DIVINE MERCY CHAPLET

Adoration of the Blessed Sacrament

Adoration, or the worship of Jesus in the Blessed Sacrament, is a very special time when we sit quietly in church and pray with Jesus. We can look at him in the Host (the bread that becomes his Body and Blood at Mass) and let our heart tell him anything we want. Remember how he asked his friends in the garden the night before he died to keep watch with him for just one hour? This is your time to do just that. It doesn't have to be a whole hour. Any amount of time you can be with Jesus is a special time.

It is a great gift to pray with Jesus in Adoration. You can use any of the prayers in this prayer book if you want, but sometimes it's helpful to have a plan that helps us pray in our own words. Here is a simple way to pray. The steps are easy to remember because they spell ACTS:

Adoration
Contrition
Thanksgiving
Supplication

Adoration

To adore God is to worship him in his power and his love. Imagine how powerful he is to create the whole universe out of nothing. His love for us is so great that he sent Jesus to be with us and to die for us. He made us and loves us! Close your eyes and know that when you are with him, you are adoring him with all the angels who surround him in the church and in heaven. They are really there with you! Think about these things as you look at Jesus on the altar. God is right there looking back at you and loving you. He really is!

Contrition

Contrition is being sorry for the things we do that hurt God or other people—things like being selfish or unkind. We should even be sorry for things we should have done but didn't—things like not being grateful for all that God and our family and friends have done for us. Have you trusted God to take care of you? If not, you can tell him you're sorry and ask him to help you trust him more.

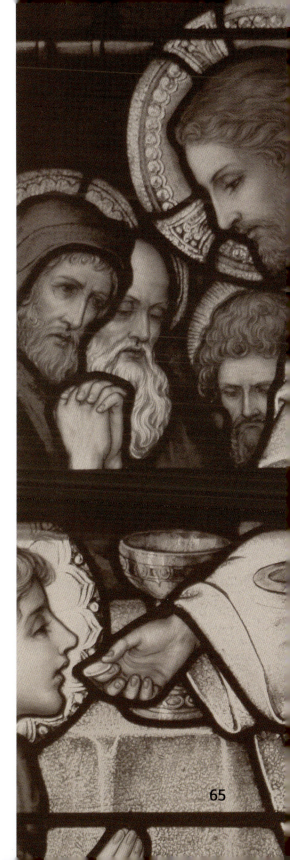

65

Thanksgiving

We should always thank God for all he has done for us: for our health, our family, our friends, his love, and the Church and the sacraments that keep us close to him. We should also be thankful for our homes where we are kept safe and for the food we have to eat. There are so many things to be thankful for.

Supplication

Supplication is just asking God for things. We can ask him to heal us or others who are sick; to help us accept our weakness; and to help others welcome us, be patient, and understand our needs. We can pray for our families and ask Jesus to bring back family members or others we may know who have left the Church. We should always pray for our world, our leaders in our government, our bishops, our priests, and the pope.

If you want to, you can end your prayer by asking God a question, like this:

> "Lord, I know that you created me for a purpose. What are you calling me to do today and every day?"

> "Lord Jesus, you know my weakness. How can my weakness help me grow closer to you each day and to come to know your will for my life?"

The most important thing to remember in a conversation with Jesus is to listen. Talk with Jesus in your heart. If you can't think of something to say, just quietly sit with him and listen for him to speak with you.

ADORATION OF THE
BLESSED SACRAMENT

If you sit quietly and love him, you can be certain that even when he seems to be silent, he is loving you back and is so happy you are spending time with him.

Part 4

Prayers for Special Times

Prayers to the Blessed Virgin Mary

Do you remember the story in the Bible of Jesus' first miracle? Here is a hint: he was at a wedding, and it involved his mother, Mary, and water and wine.

We can never forget how important Mary is. She is our mother in heaven and leads us to Jesus. We can always ask her to pray for us. She loves us very much and wants us to know Jesus better. She is happy to help us!

Saint Teresa of Kolkata (Mother Teresa) used to pray the Memorare prayer nine times in a row for a special intention. She called it her "Flying Novena." Try it, or just pray it once to ask Mary to hear a special prayer.

Memorare

Remember, O most gracious Virgin Mary,
that never was it known
that anyone who fled to your protection,
implored your help, or sought your intercession
was left unaided.
Inspired by this confidence, I fly to you,
O Virgin of virgins, my Mother;

—

to you do I come; before you I stand,
    sinful and sorrowful.
O Mother of the Word Incarnate,
    despise not my petitions,
but in your mercy hear and answer me.
Amen.

Here is a beautiful prayer that many people pray just before they go to bed. It is a very special prayer to Mary, our mother, asking her to bring us to Jesus, her Son. You pray it at the end of the Rosary.

Hail, Holy Queen

Hail, holy Queen, Mother of Mercy,
our life, our sweetness, and our hope.
To thee do we cry, poor banished children of Eve;
to thee do we send up our sighs,
mourning and weeping in this valley of tears.
Turn, then, most gracious advocate,
thine eyes of mercy toward us;
—
and after this, our exile,
show unto us the blessed fruit of thy womb, Jesus.
O clement, O loving, O sweet Virgin Mary.
Pray for us, O holy Mother of God,
that we may be made worthy of
   the promises of Christ.
Amen.

During the Easter season, you can pray this prayer instead of the Hail, Holy Queen:

Queen of Heaven

Queen of Heaven, rejoice, alleluia.
For he whom you did merit to bear, alleluia.
Has risen, as he said, alleluia.
Pray for us to God, alleluia.

Rejoice and be glad, O Virgin Mary, alleluia.
For the Lord has truly risen, alleluia.

Let us pray.
O God, who gave joy to the world
through the Resurrection of your Son,
    our Lord Jesus Christ,
grant, we beseech you,
that through the intercession of the
    Virgin Mary, his Mother,
we may obtain the joys of everlasting life.
Through the same Christ our Lord.
Amen.

Prayers that Mary Gave to the Children at Fatima

Maybe you have heard of Fatima. Some churches are named Our Lady of Fatima. Fatima is the place in Portugal where Mary appeared to three young children and asked them to pray the Rosary for peace in the world and for all those who don't believe in Jesus. It is a special thing to be able to pray the same prayers that Mary taught to these children so many years ago:

The Pardon Prayer

(given to the children at Fatima by an angel)

My God, I believe, I adore, I trust, and I love you!
    I beg pardon for those who do not believe,
    do not adore, do not trust, and do not love you.
Amen.

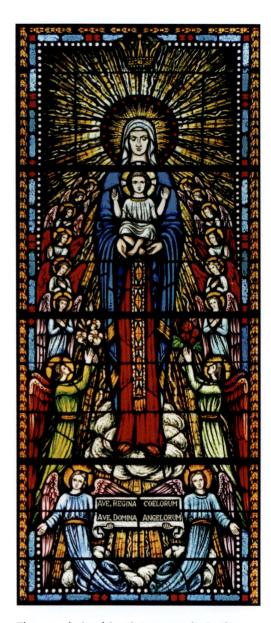

The words in this picture are in Latin and say, "Hail Queen of Heaven, Hail Lady of Angels." Mary is our Queen!

The Eucharist Prayer

(given to the children by the Blessed Mother herself)

O Most Holy Trinity, I adore you! My God, I love you in the Most Blessed Sacrament! Amen.

The Sacrifice Prayer

(another prayer given to the children by the Blessed Mother)

Oh my Jesus, I offer this for love of you, for the conversion of sinners, and to make up for the sins committed against the Immaculate Heart of Mary. Amen.

The Rosary Prayer

(another prayer given to the children by the Blessed Mother)

O my Jesus, forgive us our sins, save us from the fires of hell; lead all souls to heaven, especially those who have most need of thy mercy. Amen.

The Angel's Prayer

(another prayer given by the angel)

Most Holy Trinity—Father, Son, and Holy Spirit—
I adore you profoundly. I offer you the most
precious Body, Blood, Soul, and Divinity
of Jesus Christ, present in all the tabernacles of
the world, in reparation for the outrages,
sacrileges, and indifferences that offend him.
Through the infinite merits of his Most Sacred
Heart and the Immaculate Heart of Mary,
I beg of you to convert sinners.
Amen.

These are harder words.
"Reparation" means to
make up for something
done wrong, and a
"sacrilege" is like a crime
committed against God.

Holy Mary,
pray for us!

Angel of God, my guardian dear,
to whom God's love commits me
here. Ever this day be at my side, to
light, to guard, to rule, to guide.

Prayers to Saint Joseph

Saint Joseph was Jesus' foster father on earth. Just like he protected Jesus and Mary, we can ask him to protect us, and also for special favors. We know that he is close to Jesus in heaven and that Jesus will listen to him when he prays for us. Many people have found that these prayers to Saint Joseph are very powerful.

Traditional Prayer to Saint Joseph

O Saint Joseph, whose protection is so great,
so strong, so prompt before the throne of God,
I place in you all my interests and desires.
O Saint Joseph, help me by your powerful prayers,
and ask Jesus to grant me many spiritual
blessings so that, having asked for your heavenly
power, I may offer my thanksgiving and homage
to you, the most loving of fathers.

—

O Saint Joseph, I never get tired of thinking about
you, and Jesus asleep in your arms; I don't dare to
approach while he rests near your heart.
Press him close in my name and kiss his
fine head for me and ask him to return
the kiss when I take my dying breath.
Saint Joseph, patron of departing souls, pray for me.
Amen.

Prayer to Saint Joseph for Protection

Blessed Joseph, husband of Mary,
be with us today.
You loved and protected the Virgin,
loving the Child Jesus as your son;
when he was a baby,
you protected him from those
    who wanted to kill him.
Defend the Church, God's people,
saved by the blood of Christ.
Protector of the Holy Family,
be with us when our lives are difficult.
    —

May your prayers obtain for us
the strength to run away from what is not true
and resist the powers of evil,
so that in life we may grow in holiness
and when we die rejoice with you
    and Jesus and Mary in heaven.
Amen.

Jesus, Mary, and Joseph, I give you my heart and soul.

Prayers for Your Family

Our families are so important to us, but sometimes they are so close that we forget to pray for them. It's very important to always pray for those who are closest to us, who love us, and who take care of us.

A Prayer for My Family

O God, you are my Father in heaven.
I pray for my whole family.
Protect us and keep us safe from all
    dangers that might harm us.
Especially keep us safe from all spiritual dangers
and from doing anything that makes you sad.
Help us to never be upset or angry with one another.

—

Send your Holy Spirit to keep us strong
    in the Catholic faith.
I pray through Jesus Christ,
    your Son and my brother,
that our family will always love each other,
and that our love for Jesus will help us
    when hard things happen.
Mary, our mother, we honor you as
    the Queen of our home.
Teach us to be faithful and to love your Son,
    Jesus our King.

—

Saint Joseph, father of the Holy Family,
    keep our home free of evil,
and keep us united in love
    and service to God and one another.
Holy Family—Jesus, Mary, and Joseph—
    pray for us.
Amen.

The Holy Family,
Jesus, Mary, and Joseph,
pray for me!

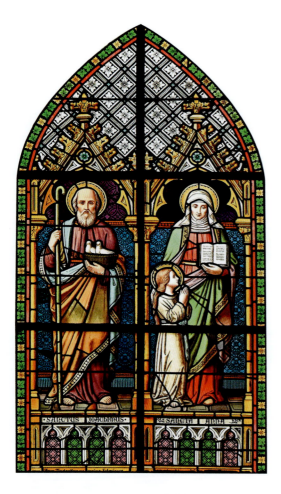

Here, we see Mary as a child with her parents, Saint Joachim and Saint Anne.

A Prayer for My Mother

Loving God, thank you for my mother.
Please bless her for her courage and her love.
Bless her for all the sacrifices
    she makes for me and my family.
Bless her for her patience and all that
    she does to make our home
a place of love where you are welcomed and adored.
Help me to always remember to tell her
    how much I love her.
Amen.

A Prayer for My Father

God, my Father in heaven,
bless my father for all he does to guide
    and support our family,
and for his love.
Keep him always close to you.
Help him to never be discouraged
    when times are hard.
Help me to always let him know how much I love him
and how much I am thankful for all he does for me.
Amen.

Prayers for Your Life's Purpose

You can be certain that God has created you for a purpose. No one is an accident. He wants you to love him and talk with him so that he can show you how to serve him. It is good to pray every day to ask Jesus what he wants you to do with the life he has given you. It may not be something big, but you can be sure it's important!

Prayer to Know Your Purpose in Life

Lord, my God and my loving Father,
you have made me to know you,
    to love you, and to serve you.
I know that you are in all things,
and that every path can lead me to you.
Of all the paths, there is one special path
    that you want me to follow.
Since I will do whatever you want me to do,
please send your Holy Spirit to me.
      —

Send him into my mind,
    to show me what you want me to do,
    and into my heart, to give me the will to do it
with all my love and with all of my strength
    for my whole life.
Jesus, I trust in you.
Amen.

Prayer to Saint Joseph to Know God's Will

O Great Saint Joseph,
you always did what God asked you to do.
Pray for me, so that I know what God wants me to do
with the life he has given me.
I know that God has a purpose for me,
and that the way to be really happy
is to find out what it is he wants me to do,
    and to do it for him.
I know how easy it is to pray
    but then still do my will and not his.
        —

Help me to not be tricked by what I want,
but to give myself completely to him and to his will.
Pray for me, dear Saint Joseph,
that I know God's will and do it every day.
Help me to choose whatever will lead me
to happiness now and in eternity.
Amen.

Even our work can become a prayer
when we offer it to Jesus.

My Jesus, I want to serve you.
I want to give my life to you.
Please show me how.

Prayers for Priests

Priests have given up many things in life to serve Jesus and his Church. They need our prayers to be strong, healthy, and faithful. It's always good to tell them thank you for what they do, and even better to pray for them often.

Prayer for Priests

God, we thank you for the gift of our priests.
Through them, we have you with us
    in the sacraments.
Help our priests to be strong in their vocation.
Help them love your people more and more.
Help them be just like Jesus.
Give them the words they need
    to spread the Gospel
and to be joyful in their ministry.
    —

Help us to see you, dear Jesus, in them.
We ask this through Jesus Christ,
who lives as our King for ever and ever.
Amen.

Prayer for More Priests and Religious in the Church

Dear God,
We pray that you will give us more
    priests and religious
to build up your Church here in my diocese.
Inspire our young men and women
by the example of so many holy priests
to give themselves totally to the work
    of Christ and his Church.
We ask this in the name of Jesus the Lord.
Amen.

Saint John Vianney

Saint John Vianney is the patron saint of parish priests. Pray to him for the priests in your parish.

Prayer of Saint John Vianney for Priests

God, please give to your Church many more priests
with a heart like yours—full of love for your people.
May they be like Christ the Good Shepherd.
May they devote themselves to prayer and penance
and be examples of humility and poverty;
shining models of holiness;

—

tireless and powerful preachers of the Word of God;
faithful dispensers of your grace in the sacraments.
May their loving devotion
to your Son Jesus in the Eucharist
    and to Mary his mother
be the source of their fruitfulness for their ministry.
Amen.

My Jesus, I love the priests in my parish. Bless them with happiness and faithfulness and help them to always be like you.

Prayers for People with Disabilities

Sometimes people struggle with having a disability. They may feel sad, anxious, or lonely. It is good to ask God to help them and remind them how much he loves them. You can also ask God to help you in your own struggles.

Prayer for People Who Are Struggling with Their Disability

My Father,
Jesus Christ cared for those
who were blind and deaf
or slow to learn.
All of us need your help,
but please give special care to those
    who have a disability,
especially me and (say names here).

May we all know the love you have for us
and come to trust in you,
through Jesus Christ.
Amen.

Prayer for Strength and Acceptance

God, my Father, I know that you created me.
I know that you have a reason for all things.
I accept the hard things in my life
and depend on you to help me accept
    my limitations as your gift.
I know that you have given all of us who love you
what we need to grow closer to you.
Help me to know that you have created
    me special and for a purpose.
Help me to accept your will in all things.

—

Help me to always show others
    how much you love me.
Help me to be patient with those who
    don't understand or may judge me.
Help me remember to always praise you
and to never be sad for what you have given me.
Please only give me what I need to love
    you more and more each day.
Bless and care for all those who care
    so lovingly for me.

—

I look forward to the day when I
    will see you in heaven
and join the saints and angels to praise you forever.
Amen.

Lord, increase my faith!
Teach me your will!

Prayers When You or Someone Else Is Sick

Sometimes, when we're sick, it is hard to pray, but it is very important to ask God to help us be well again. Here are some prayers that will help you pray when you are sick. You can also pray for others who may not feel like praying themselves.

Short Prayer for the Sick

O God, hear our prayers for those who are sick;
for those whom we ask the help of your mercy.
Send them help, O Lord, and comfort them,
that with their health restored they may thank you.
Amen.

Prayer for Someone Who Is Sick

Blessed Virgin Mary, our mother,
You watched Jesus suffer and die for
    us as you stood by his cross.
I know that you know what it means
    to suffer and to be in pain.
Pray for (say name here) who is suffering so much.
    Ask Jesus to be close to (him/her) and to help
    (him/her) trust that he loves (him/her) and
    will help (him/her) with (his/her) suffering.
Console (him/her), Mother, and help (him/her)
    to feel your love and be strong so (he/she)
    knows (he/she) is not alone.
Help me to remember to stay close to (him/her) in
    prayer and to support (him/her) however I can.
I love you, my mother.
Amen.

A Short Prayer to Mary When Sick

Mary, my mother,
I am sick and it is hard for me to pray.
Please help me to feel better soon.
My guardian angel, be with me now and help me.
Amen.

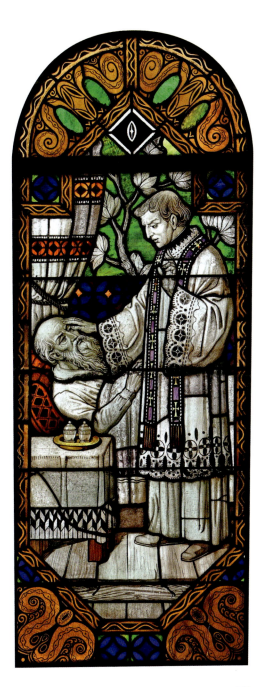

A Short Prayer to Jesus When Sick

My Jesus,
I offer my suffering to you for the salvation of souls.
Help me to accept my suffering for all
    who need prayer and healing.
Amen.

Jesus Heals a Blind Man

Jesus loves people who are sick
and wants to care for them.
We should always pray to ask
him for help and healing.

Prayers to End Abortion

When some women find out they are going to have a baby, they are very sad and afraid. They don't want their baby—sometimes especially if they find out the baby will have Down syndrome or another disability. They can make sure they don't have the baby they are carrying in their body by having an abortion. It is a very sad thing. They need us to pray for them every day so that they say yes, just like Mary did, and have their special baby to love.

Prayer for Parents When They Find Out Their Baby Has a Disability

My Jesus, I love you and I know that
    you love me just as I am.
You have created me to know you,
    to love you, and to serve you.
I ask you now to give courage to all women
who have learned that the baby they carry
    in their womb has a disability.
I know they are afraid of the future,
but I pray that they will know they can trust in you.

I pray especially for those who are considering
    aborting their baby because of fear
    or because they may think they don't
    want to have a baby with a disability.
I pray for their doctors and ask you to
    bring people into their lives
who will give them hope and help them know
that accepting a baby as your gift
    will be the best thing they could do.
    —

Help them see past their fear and have
    confidence in themselves and in you,
and in all those who love them and support them.
Amen.

Saint Gianna Molla was a doctor who loved and protected human life. When she was pregnant with her fourth child, she became very sick. Her doctors said she could abort the baby to get better, but she said no—even though she knew she might die.

Prayer for Life

(by Pope Saint John Paul II)

O Mary,
bright dawn of the new world,
Mother of the living,
to you do we entrust the cause of life.
Look down, O Mother,
upon the vast numbers
of babies not allowed to be born,
of the poor whose lives are made difficult,
of men and women
who are victims of brutal violence,
of the elderly and the sick killed
by indifference or out of misguided mercy.

Grant that all who believe in your Son
may proclaim the Gospel of life
with honesty and love
to the people of our time.

Obtain for them the grace
to accept that Gospel
as a gift ever new,
the joy of celebrating it with gratitude
throughout their lives
and the courage to bear witness to it
resolutely, in order to build,
together with all people of good will,
the civilization of truth and love,
to the praise and glory of God,
the Creator and lover of life.

Prayers When Someone You Love Has Died or Is Dying

Catholics understand death very well. We know that our prayers can help people who are dying, and even those who have already died.
There is no better gift we can give or receive than prayers at the time of death. Here are a couple to help you.

A Short Prayer to Jesus for Strength

Good Jesus,
give me a deep love for you,
so that I can be strong when I am sad.
I have lost (say name here),
and I am so sad.
Please help me be strong.
Amen.

A Prayer to Mary for Consolation

Most Holy Mary, my mother,
I have always asked you in the Hail Mary
	to pray for us
"now and at the hour of our death."
I ask now that you pray for (say name here),
that (he/she) would go peacefully
	from this world into eternity.
Please pray for me too, Mother.

	—

I don't want to say goodbye.
Help me to remember that someday
we will all be together again in eternity,
and that goodbye isn't forever.
Amen.

This is Jesus bringing Lazarus back to life. The words at the bottom mean "He cried out with a loud voice, Lazarus, come forth!"

105

Psalm 23:1–4

The LORD is my shepherd,
    I shall not want.
        He makes me lie down in
green pastures;
he leads me beside still waters;
    he restores my soul.
He leads me in right paths
    for his name's sake.

Even though I walk through the
    darkest valley,
        I fear no evil;
for you are with me;
    your rod and your staff—
        they comfort me.

Notes

- Our Father: Traditional.
- Hail Mary: Traditional.
- Glory Be: Traditional.
- Morning Prayer: Author.
- Morning Prayer to Mary: Adapted from prayer of Pope Pius IX, promulgated August 5, 1851, included in The Raccolta: Collection of Prayers and Good Works to which the Sovereign Pontiffs Have Attached Holy Indulgences, ed and trans. Sacred Congregation of Holy Indulgences (Woodstock College, MD: 1878), 219.
- Guardian Angel Prayer: Traditional.
- The Angelus: Traditional.
- Grace at Meals: Traditional.
- Night Prayer: Author.
- Saint Augustine's Prayer for Bedtime: Translation adapted from The Book of Common Prayer, Collect for Thursday Compline, 1662.
- Prayer Before Mass Begins: Author.
- Prayer at the Readings: Author.
- Prayer When the Gifts Are Brought to the Altar: Author. (inspired by the "Suscipe" of Saint Ignatius of Loyola)
- Prayer After You Receive Holy Communion: Traditional (Thomas Aquinas, "Anima Christi").
- Saying Thank You to Jesus After Mass: Author.
- A Simple Act of Faith, Hope, and Love: Author.
- Act of Faith: "Acts of Faith, Hope, and Love," United States Conference of Catholic Bishops, usccb. org. Excerpted from the Compendium of the Catechism of the Catholic Church, © Copyright 2005: Libreria Editrice Vaticana. Used by permission.

- Act of Hope: "Acts of Faith, Hope, and Love," United States Conference of Catholic Bishops, usccb.org. Excerpted from the Compendium of the Catechism of the Catholic Church, © Copyright 2005: Libreria Editrice Vaticana. Used by permission.
- Act of Love: "Acts of Faith, Hope, and Love," United States Conference of Catholic Bishops, usccb.org. Excerpted from the Compendium of the Catechism of the Catholic Church, © Copyright 2005: Libreria Editrice Vaticana. Used by permission.
- The Rosary: Traditional.
- The Divine Mercy Chaplet: Traditional.
- Memorare: Traditional.
- Hail, Holy Queen: Traditional.
- Queen of Heaven: Traditional.
- Fatima Prayers: Traditional.
- Traditional Prayer to Saint Joseph: Traditional.
- Prayer to Saint Joseph for Protection: Adapted from The Catholic Prayerbook from Downside Abbey, © David Foster, 1999, T and T Clark. Used by permission of Bloomsbury Publishing Plc.
- A Prayer for My Family: Author.
- A Prayer for My Mother: Author.
- A Prayer for My Father: Author.
- Prayer to Know Your Purpose in Life: Adapted from "Prayer to Know One's Vocation," United States Conference of Catholic Bishops, usccb.org. Used by permission.
- Prayer to Saint Joseph to Know God's Will: Traditional.
- Prayer for Priests: Adapted from "Prayer for Priests," United States Conference of Catholic Bishops, usccb.org. Used by permission.
- Prayer for More Priests and Religious in the Church: Adapted from "Prayers for Vocations,"

United States Conference of Catholic Bishops, usccb.org. Used by permission.

- Prayer of Saint John Vianney for Priests: Traditional.
- Prayer for People Who Are Struggling with Their Disability: Adapted from The Service for the Lord's Day: The Worship of God, Supplemental Liturgical Resource 1, ed. The Joint Office of Worship for the Presbyterian Church (U.S.A.) and the Cumberland Presbyterian Church (Philadelphia, PA: Westminster, 1984), 77. Used by permission.
- Prayer for Strength and Acceptance: Author.
- Short Prayer for the Sick: Adapted from The Book of Common Prayer, Order for the Visitation of the Sick, 1662.
- Prayer for Someone Who Is Sick: Author.
- A Short Prayer to Mary When Sick: Author.
- A Short Prayer to Jesus When Sick: Author.
- Prayer for Parents When They Find Out Their Baby Has a Disability: Author.
- Prayer for Life: From John Paul II, Evangelium Vitae 105, encyclical letter, March 25, 1995, vatican.va. © Dicastero per la Comunicazione - Libreria Editrice Vaticana. Used by permission.
- A Short Prayer to Jesus for Strength: Author.
- A Prayer to Mary for Consolation: Author.

Image Credits

42, 43 . . . . Richard Croft, CC BY-SA 2.0, Wikimedia
Commons.

44 . . . . . . Andreas F. Borchert, CC BY-SA 3.0 DE,
Wikimedia Commons.

Part 3

46, 49 . . . . Word on Fire.

50 . . . . . . Nheyob, CC BY 4.0, Wikimedia Commons.

51 . . . . . . Nheyob, CC BY-SA 4.0, Wikimedia Commons.

53 . . . . . . Nheyob, CC BY 4.0, Wikimedia Commons.

54 . . . . . . Word on Fire.

55 . . . . . . NateBergin, CC BY-SA 4.0, Wikimedia
Commons.

56 . . . . . . Jules and Jenny, CC BY 2.0, Wikimedia
Commons.

59, 63 . . . . Nheyob, CC BY-SA 3.0, Wikimedia
Commons.

60 . . . . . . Andreas F. Borchert, CC BY-SA 3.0 DE,
Wikimedia Commons.

65, 67 . . . . Nheyob, CC BY 4.0, Wikimedia Commons.

66 . . . . . . Nheyob, CC BY-SA 4.0, Wikimedia Commons.

Part 4

68, 71 . . . . Nheyob, CC BY-SA 4.0, Wikimedia Commons.

72 . . . . . . Nheyob, CC BY-SA 3.0, Wikimedia Commons.

74 . . . . . . Carl Huneke, CC BY-SA 4.0, Wikimedia
Commons.

75 . . . . . . Michael Kranewitter, CC BY-SA 4.0, Wikimedia
Commons.

77, 79 . . . . Nheyob, CC BY 4.0, Wikimedia Commons.

78 . . . . . . Nheyob, CC BY-SA 4.0, Wikimedia Commons.

81, 83 . . . . Andreas F. Borchert, CC BY-SA 3.0 DE,
Wikimedia Commons.

IMAGE CREDITS

There may be times when you want more than a few basic prayers to pray.

You may want to pray for someone who is sick, or for your parents, or to a saint asking for his or her help. You may be confused about your life, or you may even want to pray for your pastor, or for other people struggling with their disability. There are lots of reasons to pray.

Remember, using prayers that someone else has written is great, but there is nothing like talking with God in your own words. You may even want to write your own prayers. That would be wonderful. Try writing your own prayers on these last pages. You can also write them on a separate piece of paper and put them into this prayer book.

My Own Prayers

....

....

....

....

....

....

....

....

....

....

....

....

....

....

....

....

....

....